The Blind Lifeguard

poems by

Katrin Talbot

Finishing Line Press
Georgetown, Kentucky

The Blind Lifeguard

Any object, wholly or partially immersed in a fluid, is buoyed up by a force equal to the weight of the fluid displaced by the object.

—*Archimedes (c. 250 BC)*, in *On Floating Bodies*

Copyright © 2019 by Katrin Talbot
ISBN 978-1-63534-974-0 First Edition
All rights reserved under International and Pan-American Copyright Conventions. No part of this book may be reproduced in any manner whatsoever without written permission from the publisher, except in the case of brief quotations embodied in critical articles and reviews.

ACKNOWLEDGMENTS

"Release" was published by *Your Daily Poem*
"Supernova Remnant N132D" was performed as a theatre/dance piece by Theatre Lila in their production of *Trash*

My first memory was poolside, at three, grabbing the leg of the wrong father's trousers. Later, on the South Australian beaches, my childhood lifeguards frequently megaphoned us out of the water, on account of sharks. And, years later, as a lake lifeguard, I saved a little life, as the child's sunbathing mother slept through it all. These days, every day, the Y lifeguards get a wave of thanks from me, in their chairs above the shimmering two parts chlorine per million. These poems are about all of this; water, strokes, lives.

To save and be saved.
　　—*Katrin Talbot*

Publisher: Leah Maines
Editor: Christen Kincaid
Cover Photo: Parry Karp
Author Photo: Isabel Karp
Cover Design: Katrin Talbot with Jay Lichtmann

Printed in the USA on acid-free paper.
Order online: www.finishinglinepress.com
　　　　　also available on amazon.com

Author inquiries and mail orders:
Finishing Line Press
P. O. Box 1626
Georgetown, Kentucky 40324
U. S. A.

Table of Contents

I. SAVED

About the Sea 1
He Tells Me 2
Unexpected Blue 3
Release 4
Encounter 5
Crossing 6
The Blind Lifeguard 7
A Final Swim 8
In Need 9
A Blindwoman's Dream 10
Wanna-Be Siren 11
The Dictionary Dumpster 12
Continence 14
Today 15
Housekeeping 16
Particulate 17
As I Drag-Race Myself 18
Supernova Remnant N132D 19

II. 2PPM

Fast Girls 20
In this Box of Water 21
By Any Other Name 22
There is a Way to Bend 23
Lap 24
Add an 'S' to Mother and You Get Smother 25
The Sidewalk Diagnosis 26
Sustenance 27
I took My Soul Through the Carwash 28
Flutter Kick 29
Losing Track 30
Stroke 31
Lessons in Sinking 32
The Razor's Edge 33
Gooseberries 34
The Displacement of Water and Soul 35
On the Occasion of Your Swim Across the Strait of Gibraltar 36

I. Saved

About the Sea

It wasn't just the waves'
exhilarating embrace
and the sand's burning radiance
into our tender soles

There was also a darker lure …
the shudder inside our
young succulent bodies
as we spotted the shark's tooth
among the sea's gracious offerings,
as we thought of Them

Out There
swift, straight
and impossibly smooth
like the teeth we
held and stroked

We knew they were there.
There, we'd cleared the waters
for them many a time,
wondering always if that really
made a solid case
for them to find
a bloodier pasture

No need to mention
the underwritten
power of the surf …
the sharks were It
Even as we ate them,
the redolent fish and chips,
out of the greasy newspaper wrappings,
they won

They always do.

He Tells Me
—in memory of Howard Karp

that Brahms
had such a fear.
Water,
bodies of water

His work,
bodies of repertoires
filled with treacherous leaps,
spear points of flats,
frightening modulations that
only a bold hand and fearless heart
could compose

He couldn't swim.
Crossing the Channel to
accept honorary degrees from
Cambridge, Oxford,
seemed impossible.

"I can sympathize," sighed the
story-teller, my children's grandfather,
who had sighed with relief as
each strong girl learned to swim,
joined the team,
forgot how to
sink

Unexpected Blue

A non-Picasso blue,
rebel to the weather forecast.
this morning of light,
when gray was expected.
armor on, inside plans
drawn up already—the rains
imperative for
spring cleaning

Wishing I could bottle up this
kind of blue, a summer batch of
sky kombucha, to give as a
present to myself,
or to all those whose
bassline is a
dark pewter in
this formidable world

Release

It is now February in a
Northern State
and the garlic chive ghost just
outside the window still
holds its seeds,
even after blizzards, rains,
winds of such unsettling

Like an orphanage, now,
for hard little griefs,
nestled in their paper cradles,
shiny in their resilience,
waiting for the reluctant
release, not yet ready to
settle into an unfurled heart,
drop the pretense of eternity
and get to the work of
breaking
open

Encounter

The swim I swim is out in
the deeper part of the Bay,
where fish are seldom seen,
and when they are, they're
five inches, max
SO IMAGINE MY SURPRISE
THIS MORNING
when a yard-long creature
swam swiftly beneath me
and all I could think was
LARGE DORSAL FIN
until I saw how flat the fish was,
a strayed albacore,
and I returned to my heartbeat and
my surface task
of breathing,
of living,

grateful

The Big Island, Hawaii

Crossing

On the drive out to my river,
the one I don't own
yet claim a few times a year
with a desperate need to see
a powerful flow,
I remind myself how to live a
let go life as I fly along the highway,
protractor straight,
even over the glacial hills

Yet the little crosses along stretches
brand themselves into my cartwheel mind,
the markers of mortality,
reminding us of Error

A new one, this year, right on
the beach, under the bridge;
my companion tells me with tight lips
that last summer it was a drowning,
a bad one, on this beach where all the signs
say CAUTION
strong undercurrent,
but who would believe that of a sweet Wisconsin river
on a lovely summer afternoon?

Piranhas in paradise,
rattlesnakes along the trail.
Read the signs.
Know your place in
the society of nature

The Blind Lifeguard

She did *pro bono* work only,
her ears telescopic between
mosquito and a gasp

She had learned to swim in the
ocean without the fear of sandy
shadows below that catch
the sighted

In her dreams,
for she had held the big shells
with their blind tunnels,
and knew a beautifully-built board by touch,
she surfed on mango pits through
clouds of silent cities,
and awoke to the tide's announcements,
returning to her hueless days

Her sister had taken her on her board out
past the surf's treble to the swells
–she'd sit on the board's whale back
and fly through a watery realm.
Sometimes they'd find a dolphin she'd fall onto
and let it lead the dance

On stormy days, when the beach
shuddered under a whipped flag,
she would find patterns
in the raindrops' window riots,
count the surf's noble secrets,
one crash at a time.

But on quiet days, she was
the tower's ears, teamed
with the binoculars,
winnowing through to
a lung's discordant song

A Final Swim

It was a good morning to die if
you were at the end of your season like
the prairie plants slowly
burning dark into their destinies,
the seeding staged, the green fade
in the dewy field

I went down to the water,
gazed at the lily pads holding
down the pond
and caught a twirling
on the surface—
A winged something
too far for me to save
A beautiful desperate
choreography, etching
ripples across the pewter surface
I hoped for a hungry fish to
end its frantic spin,
but no-one came,
so I did the only thing I could do:
witness a beautiful
demise

In Need

She sits within the phrase
on a throne of frustration,
the ancient king inside ready to fight,
the princess asleep by the sword, the temporal pain
a cloud, a curse,
a label

Only her patience will win the battle,
wake the armoured maiden

And I say,
let the loons cheer her on,
those beautiful sharp creatures,
with a wild laugh,
let the gulls encourage with
sad screams
And when she steps on the inevitable acorn,
let its massive potential
shudder up through her boots and
strengthen her belief in
her own
fortitude,
put the word *discouraged* in a
soft cage in a dark closet,
close the howling door behind
her

A Blindwoman's Dream

Maybe I dreamt it when
just in love, or
just out of love, when
the subconscious
rules and wrangles
with the off-balance
conscience
Nevertheless,
a sightless world
held me tightly
and fed me only
maps
Sometimes, for pudding,
3-D topologicals,
where my fingers could
slide across plains
snake along rivers
bump along mountain ranges
and, if I piloted
two trembling hands,
I could slide into
a pacific, an atlantic,
in the same swim
with no fear of sharks, depths, storms,
embracing a continent
in a random journey without weather,
without lion, tiger, bear,
safe, for now,
in my blinding freedom

Wanna-Be Siren

What would you say
if you were to
know the real me,
the one whose smiles blind,
whose embrace is

the first step towards a
suffocating certain,
whose wink sparks
fire across those prairies of
presumed innocence,
and finally,
the power of my
crocodile tears—
their sting, their final
pull under into that
rippling world
beneath

The Dictionary Dumpster

Some obsolete words can be found
huddled in shame
beneath a pile of derivatives,
brushing alphabet dandruff
off their shoulders,
while others have had their last laughs
cryogenically frozen and are always
happy to show them off

As far as specific extinctions,
I'm pretty sure there was a shattering,
or at least a lunar eclipse
when the word *nithing*
(a contemptible or despicable person)
gave up the ghost

And who wouldn't shiver about
the 'fear of change' in the old spelling
—*kainotophobia*?

Quidnunc ended up eating itself—
an inquisite, gossipy person has no life of
his or her own in the end

Speaking of eating, *Groak*
(to watch in silence as others eat)
can be found in a corner,
waiting for the rats to finish,
pining for an invitation to
join in the gnawing

And the word *Queerplungers*
sank in shame,
once the Humane Society for
the Recovery of Drowned Persons
caught onto those who faked
their drowning to allow

accomplices a guinea per
saved body

The word *Lunting*, however,
(walking while smoking a pipe)
has turned out to be inextinguishable
and in the evenings, can be found
strolling along the dumpster rim,
releasing fragrant Lilliputian puffs to
perfume the slight stench
of expiring words
in the soft, lettered
twilight

Continence

There's a word to
have as a side
at the breakfast table
a word placed next to
the pleasant eggs,
the supportive toast

A word that's chewy,
filled with gristle,
but…
toothsome

You can chew the self
restraint of it
and spit it out,
yielding to impulse or desire
all in a single
bite

Today, in the snow
that has become a curse,
the cold that has become a killer,
I will design something

Not a plot to
overthrow the government
but maybe one to
overthrow winter

I will snip away
at reams of paper,
fashioning snowflake
after snowflake
and then I will build
microclimate-changing
bonfire with them

And the Aussie still inside me
shall do a black swan dance
around the ring of fire

Housekeeping
> *... and fold my soul forever in thy own*
> —*Trumbull Stickney*

I have shelves of them,
but they are mostly
expired,
according to their labels

I've organized them in stacks
according to their lack of 's
A. Rigidity
B. Serendipity
C. Malleability
And, once re-organized,
I check on them
every seven years or so,
when the itch returns

Particulate

It seems so relevant
without a microscope
after a swim
in crashing surf
when sand particles
announce themselves
in your scalp
when you jog fingers
through sun-bleached hair

As you lie upon the beach,
you begin to think of the
oxygen atoms your lungs
reached for in the submersions,
and then the bits of sand,
become, in your sun-dazed
peaceful mind of a mind,
behemoth structures
holding up your
solar system-sized body,
and you slip into
a light dream, as the seagulls
scrape through your dozing with
their piercing avian
conversations

As I drag-race myself
down Memory Lane,
I slam the brakes on
1979, on a beach
where you, in your first prime,
muscles, tan, smile—
you, my gravity as
your exquisite shadow
engulfed mine with
the kind of dark that
sustained me,
warm, protective, even
at highnoon when we lost
our delineation

Supernova Remnant N132D

Maybe that's where my
heart is,
on those dark days,
drawn to the expanding
remnant of a
star explosion.
So close to our sorrows,
aren't they?
A quick dance with
hydrogen and oxygen,
a tango with what remains when
something shatters, a reminder and a
rejuvenation, then back to heart's
task of pulsing, sustaining,
before the next
unexpected
rive

II. 2ppm*

*the concentration of chlorine in a standard swimming pool: two parts per million

Fast Girls

Some of us would, high schoolers,
work out with
the college men, different lanes, but the
pace was set,
the pool a pure churning

If you have never heard the unvoiced
power of a swimteam's mid-workout,
imagine a roar of surf without
an ocean's beat; that is the sound that
fills a pool's chamber

But this poem isn't about
muscle and endurance
It's about
the new light-yellow Speedo's
issued to the college men
How we had to imagine
placing our chins
on a high wide shelf and not
looking down
when we spoke to them,
how we let our goggles get extra foggy
so we wouldn't be disappointed
with the promised land, in those Speedos
that left nothing, maybe, to the imagination
of a bashful
fourteen-year-old
girl

In this box of water,
I swim along a side
of the rectangle,
flip against another,
and push towards
the next boundary,
as if I were assigned
to weave tightly a
thin strip in a
tapestry of effort,
with a flecking of
late afternoon golds
on cloudless laps

By Any Other Name

As awkward as I felt—
high school, oh god—
so tall, so skinny,
so swimteam,
hair shiny-almost-green,
when the French class
door closed, we became our
French names:
we were older,
more elegant, civil, beautiful,
as I would carry the grace of
Angelique through the next hour,
even past it on a good day,
as Madame Hewitt
pulled us slowly and gracefully through
her beloved language,
participle by participle,
her pursed and painted lips
our portal into
what must have
been

There is a way to
bend towards a duty
that can feel beautiful—
the task of the old monk
drying eggplant,
the cleaners at the Y
mopping against
the constant influx of
muddy bootprints,
the crossing guard's judgment of
which car should stop

Their silent chant like
shadows that bend across
an uneven land,
that sketch
the forgiving
curve

Lap

The month I swam two point
two seven miles a day,
my mind full of numbers,
divisions, fractions,
while the sum total
loomed just ahead of
my next stroke,
like a crown,
like a jagged peak
as I pulled my way
across the mileage,
a chlorinated yard at a time

There's a shimmer in
the strength of commitment,
a weightless glow
you can carry into
the rest of your
day in a month of flipturns,
of three thousand yards
times thirty

Add an 'S' to Mother and You Get Smother

I just remember him as
the swim team kid with a
jockstrap under his suit

I don't clearly recall the mother
but I do remember the explanation
that his mother insisted on it,
which meant we all
stared when we would have
otherwise not

So I wonder if he's
made it through life ok,
successfully siring grandchildren
for her, or if he ended up
a woman-hater dreaming of
matricide every other
Tuesday

Intentions when context was
not considered,
and the Greek chorus was
filled with
middle-schoolers

The Sidewalk Diagnosis

'You're a nester,' he said,
stopped me along a
busy concrete wayfair

Back in grad school,
I would have been wearing
gold hoop earrings,
lab-bench-acid-burned jeans
before they were cool,
an old sweater

I don't remember any details
from Mr. Insight, just the label;
he was right
Should I have chased him,
courted him?
Maybe it was simply my long braid
of shiny swimmer's hair,
perfect for adding the golden touch to
any nest from a
life lived in four countries,
where belongings were
hard to hold onto,
in the way a move
dilutes and concentrates,
regardless of distance

Sustenance

> *I am like a mad woman*
> *who has been caught eating pearls*
> —Tess Gallagher

I watched a jeweler
bite my strand of pearls—
just opened her mouth and
chomped, a shocking technique
for a young bride to witness
but of course, when I got home,
I nibbled

But were I mad,
the lustrous mass of
oyster imperfection
would not be my
appetizer of choice
The strands of river pearls
my daughter gave me,
dancing all day around my wrist,
staring at me like tiger eyes,
those, I'd suck on one by
one until I finally became
a river, fierce and
round the bend

I took my soul through
the car wash yesterday
Of course I drove the convertible—
we both love the water dance,
the spinning,
the bubbles

Oh the suds
like sunshine when
storms are expected
And the tickle of
the swinging car mops

Anyway,
it was exhilarating
and afterwards,
my soul, who is ancient,
but of few words,
screamed,
'Again!'

Flutter Kick

As we readied ourselves
after our swim for
December's outside world,
she told me
she was understudy for
the Sugar Plum Fairy,
and, so critical during
the Nutcracker run,
that the pool thankfully
forced her feet out of first position
as the kickboard
drove her release

I'd be in the pit, I told her,
but, sadly, wouldn't see her

The necessary understudy:
adjunct professor
vice prez
sub-list viola
as we are placed by
luck, by determination,
by need,
our roles strong and critical,
quietly woven into
the general-use tapestry,
in the area adjacent to
threads of delicate
gold

Losing Track

Right outside the Lost & Found bin
in the Y locker room
a pair of little pink cowboy boots
stood at attention,
at inattention, I suppose,
waiting for the relief of claiming,
the return to the making of
little exclamation points in
the snow, lines and lines of them,
a sketch of how owning a pair
of little pink cowboy boots
must feel

Stroke

She was teaching us
the frog kick, part of
the elusive coordination,
in a dimly-lit old pool,
subzero temps waiting outside to
embrace us, slay us,
after swim lessons

And because of the stroke's name,
and because our instructor had just
had a baby, I could not
ignore the eye-level bosom,
white, massive, mapped
with lapis veins,
as she held my kickboard
as I thought of frogs and babies

And when I finally harnessed
the kick to the stroke.
I was a frog on a bicycle, flying
towards that freedom from sinking,
towards a shoebox of future medals,
the glide,
my self-hitched chariot ride,
my flat breast-plate
shining

Lessons in Sinking

After the mile,
I want to float it out in an
Ophelian moment, then
sink into
the embrace of submission

I can't.
I float to the top

Meanwhile,
in the lane next to me,
little ones are learning
to battle fears,
to defy the sinking,

as I watch their
tiny feet churn towards
Almost

The Razor's Edge

I recall it was about
not nicking our lovely legs
with a bumbling novice shave,
but my twin and I watched, impatiently,
as other swim team girls entered,
one by one, the mother-coached
Smooth Leg Club as
we waited and waited, with our
long, long fuzzy legs, for
the maternal starting gun,
the gate to open, in the slow motion
race towards
Woman

Gooseberries

Age Eight,
my first memory of them,
as I emerged from a
long, numbing swim in Lake Superior,
a galaxy away from my Australian beach,
so cold I couldn't
stop swimming
in that parallel freezing universe,
knowing my strokes only by sound,
my skinny biceps anesthetized, my toes
the first to go
And out of the water, into a sun-smooched towel,
gazing at the carton of translucent green breasts,
at the little Canadian planets of
tartness

The Displacement of Water and Soul

*I was like a glove turned inside out,
how it becomes the other hand—Frank X. Gaspar*

In the countryness of
Oblique, you might
find us, the immigrants
who had not suffered
but floated towards in
decent accommodation

We weave ourselves into
society, culture,
surprising with our
origin bios,
the unexpected twist
in pronounciation,
the odd habits with
forks and then
knives,
our eyes always open,
scanning for
how to's and this way,
trying to, with a seemingly
apathetic earnestness,
to fit
in

On the Occasion of Your Swim Across the Strait of Gibraltar
for Gretchen Talbot, my twin sister

I hold you in my shaking hand,
watching on the phone
as you power towards
our evolution,
the one where we
leave the water,
crawl onto the
Land
and take in the
new world,
the one After
the Crossing

www.ingramcontent.com/pod-product-compliance
Lightning Source LLC
LaVergne TN
LVHW041311080426
835510LV00009B/952